AN APPROACH TO FOOD COSTING

AN APPROACH TO
Food Costing

RICHARD KOTAS

B.Com., M.Phil., A.C.I.S.
Department of Hotel and Catering Management,
University of Surrey

BARRIE & JENKINS
COMMUNICA-EUROPA

© 1960 by Richard Kotas

First published 1960 by
Barrie and Jenkins Ltd
24 Highbury Crescent
London N5 1RX

Reprinted 1965
Second Edition (revised) 1973
Reprinted 1976

ISBN 0 214 66863 0

Printed in Great Britain by
Fletcher & Son Ltd, Norwich

CONTENTS

PREFACE

This compact book has been written with the object of providing a simple and, as far as possible, comprehensive introduction to food costing. It is hoped that it will meet the requirements of students and—to some extent—supervisors and managers in the hotel and catering industry.

An endeavour has been made to present the main principles involved, rather than methods in use in particular sections of the industry. It is hoped, therefore, that *AN APPROACH TO FOOD COSTING* will be of value to those aspiring to supervisory and managerial posts not only in hotels and restaurants but also in other branches of catering—hospital catering, industrial catering, institutional catering, clubs, etc.

I desire to express my indebtedness to all those who have, in one way and other, helped in the preparation of this introductory volume. In particular, I wish to express my thanks to the former Head of the Hotel and Catering Management Department, Battersea College of Technology, Mr. John Fuller, F.H.C.I., M.R.S.H., A.F.G.I., for his encouragement and valuable suggestions. I also owe a great debt to my colleague, Mr. S. Medlik, B.Com., F.R.Econ.S., for reading the manuscript and for his help with the chapter on Profit; also, to Mr. B. E. Davis, M.H.C.I., for his help in the preparation of the exercises on material costing.

The prices used in the problems and exercises—particularly those relevant to Chapter Three—present a minor problem. Although they are revised and up-dated now and again, they cannot always reflect current market realities. Fortunately, however, this is a matter which does not invalidate the basic methods of control or the principles involved.

London 1976   R.K.

CHAPTER ONE

INTRODUCTION

The development of cost accounting and costing methods has been a long and evolutionary process—a process proceeding side by side with industrial development.

The beginning of the twentieth century witnessed a great competition resulting from the introduction of new machinery and the extension of national and world markets. This made it imperative for each and every business enterprise to search for improved methods of production and ways and means of reducing costs. Similarly it became necessary to know the precise cost of each process and every article produced: hence the necessity for cost and sales analysis and information for management—the two main functions of costing.

Much progress has recently been made in food costing methods and control procedures in this industry. Much, however, remains to be done, particularly in smaller hotels and catering establishments many of which appear to have shown little enthusiasm for some of the new costing techniques and control procedures.

How, then, can we explain the caterer's hesitance in introducing costing? It seems that there have been two major factors operating against the development of costing

1

in this industry : firstly, the structure of the Hotel and catering industry and secondly, the complexity of hotel and catering operation.

THE STRUCTURE OF THE INDUSTRY

A prominent feature of the hotel and catering industry is the relatively small size of the average establishment which does not permit any great degree of specialization. Specialization, however, is an important prerequisite of the evolution of new techniques and efficient methods.

Further, the industry still relies on a fairly high proportion of cheap, unskilled labour, which has a disincentive effect on the introduction of new machinery and improved techniques.

Finally, facilities for supervisory and management training in the hotel and catering industry, though considerably improved in the last ten years or so, are still rather inadequate.

THE COMPLEXITY OF HOTEL AND CATERING OPERATION

The very nature of hotel keeping and catering presents a number of problems to the cost accountant as well as to management at the top. The main factors which render the application of costing methods difficult may be summarized as follows :

(a) Daily variations in the assortment and size of production necessitating daily planning of production and sales.

(b) The rapidity with which transactions take place, resulting in a high rate of stock turnover.

(c) The fact that most transactions are small in amount.

(d) Impossibility of storage of products over lengthy periods of time. (In the case of hotels and motels and similar establishments the storage of the most important ' product '—accommodation—is impossible!).

(e) The extensive use of internal by-products.

The application of costing in hotels is in certain respects even more difficult than in the case of other catering establishments. Unlike the industrial canteen, the average hotel provides the guest with a great number of services: food, drink, accommodation, laundry, valet services, etc. In some hotels the visitor finds on the premises a travel agency, florist, gift shop and other services.

To sum up, from the costing point of view one must regard the hotel as an undertaking composed of a number of 'production centres' each of which (excepting the ancillary departments, for example, plate room, stores) provides the visitor with a different type of service.

COSTING DEFINED

Cost accounting may be defined as the analysis of income and expenditure for the purpose of determining the cost of each product, service and department and the contribution that each of these makes to the total profit of the business. The second main objective of costing is to produce adequate information for the management of the business for control purposes.

A comprehensive system of costing must necessarily cover the whole range of items produced and sold and enable the caterer to ascertain the cost of, and hence the profit on, each item sold.

THE OBJECTS AND ADVANTAGES OF COSTING

It is obvious that for the purpose of efficient management financial accounting in itself is in many ways inadequate—both as a system of control and as a source of information.

The main object of financial accounts is to disclose whether or not a profit has been made by the establishment as a whole. A progressive hotelkeeper would certainly not be satisfied with a single figure of net profit at the end of an accounting period, and would at least require to know the profit made by each revenue-producing department of the business.

The advantages of costing may be summarized as follows:
(a) A system of costing discloses the net profit made by each revenue-producing department and shows the cost of each meal produced. Similarly, it enables the hotelkeeper to determine the profit made on the sale of accommodation.
(b) An efficient system of costing will reveal possible sources of economies and thus result in a more rational utilization of labour, stores, etc.
(c) Costing provides valuable information necessary for the adoption of a sound price policy.
(d) Cost records facilitate the speedy quotation for special functions such as wedding receptions and banquets.
(e) Finally, cost accounting must be regarded as an important instrument in the hands of the management.

Costing is frequently thought of as merely a cost-finding device. It is important to remember, however, that the determination of cost is only one function of costing. The importance of costing lies in the information it makes available to the management of the establishment rather than in its cost-finding function. It is clear, however, that the fulfilment of the second function depends on the efficient discharge of the first.

It follows, therefore, that costing must provide actual figures of cost for the purpose of comparison with previous trading periods; costing must furnish the management with interim (weekly or monthly) Profit and Loss Accounts; finally, the management having delegated responsibility to the supervisors and the staff, must be periodically informed of current performance. The cost accountant must, therefore, evolve objective standards for the measurement of performance and report on current results.

INTRODUCTION OF A COSTING SYSTEM

It is essential to realize that no one system of costing will suit each and every catering business. No two catering establishments are identical and before a costing system is introduced a great deal of thought must be devoted to the general organization of the business. It is necessary to ensure that the following conditions are satisfied when a costing system is being installed :

(a) The first and foremost condition is the co-operation of all the departments concerned. It is as well to remember that the costing system must be adapted to the general pattern of organization and not *vice versa*. It is a well-known fact that any attempt to alter the accepted procedures in an establishment causes resentment and, as a result, the full co-operation of certain departments is not always secured.

(b) Second in the order of importance is the simplicity of the system. Where records have to be compiled by staff, full instructions, preferably in writing, must be issued. The amount of clerical labour involved must be kept down to the minimum.

The reader will realize that it is impossible to obtain satisfactory results from any system without some trouble and expense. It is a fact, however, that catering establishments which have introduced costing have found that the cost of the system is by no means disproportionate to the benefits derived.

CHAPTER TWO

THE ELEMENTS OF COST

The first function of costing—the analysis of income and expenditure—would be impossible without some method of cost classification.

In order to arrive at the total cost of any one meal or service it is necessary to analyse the total of expenditure under several distinct headings.

Basically the total cost of every product consists of three main elements:

1. Materials (Food Cost)
2. Labour $\Big\}$ = TOTAL COST
3. Overheads.

In catering it is usual to express each element (component) of cost as a percentage of the selling price. This method of cost analysis has been found useful mainly because it permits the caterer to control his profit margins and thus secure an equitable return on the capital invested in his establishment.

COSTS AND PROFITS

We may now explain the basic relationships between costs, profits and sales.

Kitchen Profit Kitchen profit (gross profit) may be defined as the difference between sales and the cost of materials used or food cost:

$$\text{Sales} - \text{Food Cost} = \text{Kitchen Profit}$$

Net Profit Net profit may be defined as the difference between sales and total cost:

$$\text{Sales} - \text{Total Cost} = \text{Net Profit}$$

The reader will, of course, appreciate that it is possible to derive a number of equations from those shown immediately above, for example:

Kitchen Profit — (Labour + Overheads) = Net Profit
Kitchen Profit + Food Cost   = Sales

KITCHEN PROFIT AND NET PROFIT

Note: It will be observed that kitchen wages are not taken into account when calculating Kitchen Profit; kitchen wages as well as the wages paid in other departments are part of the total cost of labour. Labour and overheads are deducted from Kitchen Profit to arrive at Net Profit.

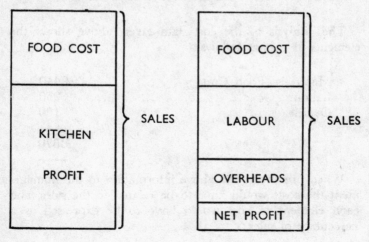

AN ILLUSTRATION

Let us now illustrate this method of cost analysis by means of a simple example.

The cost records of the Hampton Court Restaurant show the following items of expense for the month of July, 19..:

Rent and Rates	£55
Lighting and Heating	20
Wages—Kitchen	120
Wages—Restaurant	130
Printing and Stationery	10
Insurance	5
Sundry Office Expenses	20
Depreciation	70
Materials (Food Cost)	440
TOTAL	£870

Sales for July £1,030
Number of Customers served—*4,847*.

The analysis of the cost data given above shows the elements of cost as follows:

Materials (Food Cost)	£440
Labour	250
Overheads	180
	£870

When presenting the above information to the management the costs would have to be related to the sales, and each element of cost would have to be expressed as a percentage of sales:

Materials (Food Cost)	£440	42·7%
Labour	250	24·3%
Overheads	180	17·5%
Net Profit	160	15·5%
SALES	£1,030	100·0%

From the percentages shown above it follows that out of every £1·00 worth of sales 42·7p goes into food costs, 24·3p into labour costs, 17·5p into overheads and 15·5p remains as net profit of the business. This may be represented by means of a simple diagram as shown below.

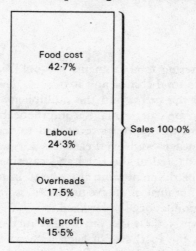

We know that during the period covered by the foregoing cost information the restaurant served 4,847 customers, which enables us to calculate the average spending power for July.

$$\frac{\text{TOTAL SALES}}{\text{NO. OF CUSTOMERS}} \quad \frac{£1,030}{4,847} = 21·3\text{p}$$

Analysis of Average Spending Power. We have now determined the composition of total sales for July, and this enables us to assess the contribution each customer makes to the costs of the business and the net profit.

The calculation would be as follows:

Materials (Food Cost)	$= 0\cdot213 \times 42\cdot7 = 9\cdot1$p
Labour	$= 0\cdot213 \times 24\cdot3 = 5\cdot2$p
Overheads	$= 0\cdot213 \times 17\cdot5 = 3\cdot7$p
Net Profit	$= 0\cdot213 \times 15\cdot5 = 3\cdot3$p

Average Spending Power   21·3p

TOTAL COST

In most catering establishments it would be impossible to ascertain the total cost of any item sold. The great number of items on the menu and the multiplicity of the services rendered by the caterer make it impracticable to apportion to each item an appropriate charge to recover the total cost of the wages and overheads. As a result the methods of costing adapted in the hotel and catering industry must necessarily be different from those used in other industries, where the number of items produced is frequently quite small and production standardized.

Consequently the most practicable method of costing is to ascertain the food cost of each item on the menu and:
(a) control the Kitchen Profit on each meal served and total Kitchen Profit,
(b) control total labour and total overheads without attempting to apportion them to individual items produced or services rendered.

The reader will, of course, realize that the procedure outlined above has a number of limitations and therefore lends itself to a number of criticisms. The most important point of criticism is that the customer pays not only for the cost of the materials used but also for the other two elements of cost—the wages and overheads.

A low food-cost item may be quite costly in terms of labour or overheads or both. Hence, the argument runs, it just isn't good enough to cost in terms of one element of cost only. It is, however, only in isolated cases that we can with any degree of certainty calculate the cost of the wages, for example, for functions, wedding receptions, banquets.

CHAPTER THREE

MATERIALS (FOOD COST)

MATERIAL COSTING

Material costing has a number of purposes. Its first object is to ascertain the food cost of particular items on the menu; also to ascertain the total expenditure on food over a period of time. The latter quantity has, of course, a significance of its own, but it is also of immense value when expressed in relation to the volume of business.

The ascertainment of food cost is not an end in itself. It is only of value in so far as it helps the caterer to control his costs, prices and profit margins and provides information necessary for the formulation of his policy.

Food cost control must necessarily occupy a prominent place in food costing, and that mainly for two reasons : first because in most catering establishments the expenditure on food amounts to as much as half the total cost; also because this component of cost lends itself to being varied as a matter of policy to a far greater extent than do the wages or the overheads.

An effective system of material costing will disclose faulty purchasing, inefficient storing and the installation of such a system is a powerful psychological factor which tends to prevent waste and petty pilfering.

Finally, another object of material costing is to ensure consumer satisfaction. A system of material costing will help the caterer to ensure that the customer is given adequate food value for his money and is not left at the mercy of the caterer's staff.

PURCHASE AND HANDLING OF STORES

The purchase, handling and consumption of stores involve a number of specialist functions and have many aspects, some of which, important as they are, fall outside the province of costing. The cost accountant is interested in this general problem mainly because of its bearing on the economical utilization of the establishment's resources.

Purchasing In most medium-sized and small establishments the authority to purchase provisions is vested in the manager or his assistant. In some of the larger establishments it is delegated to the buyer or the chef or the catering officer. Whoever is responsible for the buying of provisions it is clear that the person responsible can greatly contribute to the successful running of the business by the proper discharge of his duties.

The size of the order as indeed the size of the stock carried, both influence running costs. The size of the order will always depend on a number of factors such as, for instance, the following :

(a) Existing stocks.
(b) The expected volume of business.
(c) The number of staff employed.
(d) Current market prices and current trends.

It is, of course, a truism to say that a certain amount of stock must be held at all times, but it must also be realized that over-buying invariably involves the establishment in a certain amount of expense. Over-buying results in loss of interest on the capital which has been invested in excessive, idle stocks; valuable storage space must be provided and the risk of loss through deterioration is always present.

Volume Forecasting. Much progress has recently been made in techniques relating to the purchasing of food and food preparation. Perhaps the most important new technique introduced in this area is that of volume forecasting.

The main objective of volume forecasting is to predict

how many customers will have meals in the establishment and what they are going to choose from the menu. We thus have to predict two main things:

(a) The number of customers for lunch, dinner, etc., for each day of the week.

(b) Their choice of menu items. If we predict that 100 customers will come for lunch, we may decide that only 80 will take the first course and that of these 20 will ask for melon, say 15 for tomato soup, 25 for smoked salmon, etc.

Naturally predictions of this kind are not easy. It helps if one keeps what is known as *sales histories*, showing for each menu item how many portions have been sold over a period of time. Another helpful device is *cyclic menus*. If the cycle extends over 14 days, we start with the menu for day 1 and, so to speak, carry on until day 14, after which we revert to day 1; and so on. Where cyclic menus are used it is quite usual to observe distinct patterns both in the total number of covers and the relative popularity of various menu items; and this is of course of great help in volume forecasting.

One of the important advantages of volume forecasting is that it enables the caterer to put his purchasing on a sound basis. Having made the two predictions we can convert the menu items shown in the volume forecast into raw material equivalents and order from the suppliers accordingly. It will be appreciated that this applies to the perishables rather than the non-perishables.

Where volume forecasting has been introduced it has usually been found that stock levels are lower. Of course what matters most of all is the idea that we should be buying the food which is needed for the meals that the customers will require. Volume forecasting should, therefore, be regarded as an important link between customers' preferences and the purchasing of food.

Receipt of Stores   On delivery the incoming goods must be checked for both quantity and quality and particulars thereof entered in a Goods Received Book (see page 16). In the case of perishable goods it is particularly essential to check the quality, since bad quality may well double the cost to the establishment of the commodity in question. If the quality is found unsatisfactory for one reason or another the matter must immediately be taken up with the suppliers.

Once the goods have been received into the stores they become the responsibility of the storekeeper. There is no doubt that from the costing point of view the stewardship of the stores is a major responsibility.

ACCOUNTING FOR STORES

The system to be adopted in the stores will naturally depend on a number of factors such as the size of the establishment, and the data which it is intended the system should provide. Clearly, whatever the circumstances, each establishment ought to have some sort of system; otherwise the best results will not be achieved.   There are two main methods of stores accounting :

Bin Cards   To facilitate the maintenance of this system the stores should be kept in appropriate drawers, bins or other receptacles. For each item there is kept a separate record on a bin card (see page 22) showing the description of the commodity, receipts, issues and the balance. It is advantageous to show the minimum stock in order to facilitate the ordering of further supplies.

Stock Books   An alternative to bin cards is to keep stock books. These should preferably be kept on the loose-leaf principle—a bound book is not recommended. Under this system a card (see pages 21 & 22) is kept for each item showing the same information that would be recorded on a bin card.

GOODS RECEIVED BOOK

DATE	SUPPLIER	Order No	DESCRIPTION	QT.	REMARKS

The data recorded on bin cards or in the stock book would be in terms of physical quantities rather than values. There is, of course, no reason at all why the values, in addition to the quantities, should not be shown. It is considered, however, that this might involve too much clerical labour having regard to the value of the additional information derived.

PRICING OF ISSUES

Wherever there is a system of food requisitioning by means of written stores requisitions, there must be some method of pricing such issues. The method of pricing the food issued from the stores depends mainly on the type of commodity in question.

Perishables In the case of perishables it is usual to price the issues on the basis of actual purchase prices. Where the stock of an item consists of several separate lots, delivered at different prices, an average price should be taken.

Non-Perishables In the case of non-perishables, one of several different methods may be adopted :
(a) Where market fluctuations are frequent it is best to work on the basis of an average price.
(b) In the case of slow-moving, infrequently purchased items the actual purchase price may be taken as the basis.
(c) Finally, it is possible to price the issues at current market prices; this method would however involve additional clerical labour.

It is suggested that in most small and medium-sized catering establishments it would be convenient to apply the actual purchase-price method in the case of perishable provisions, and the average-price method in the case of non-perishables.

The importance of accurate methods for the pricing of issues need hardly be emphasized. Where physical stock-taking takes place at quarterly or half-yearly intervals, the priced requisitions may be used as the basis for the calculation of the weekly or monthly food cost. The preparation of weekly or monthly trading accounts is thus very much facilitated.

If the issues are priced accurately, then :

Opening Stock + Purchases — Closing
Stock = Total of Priced Requisitions

In practice it is always found that there is a certain amount of difference between the total of priced requisitions and the cost of food consumed found upon stock-taking. The main causes of such differences are : short- and over-issues, petty pilfering, inaccurate pricing and evaporation.

STOCK-TAKING

In addition to the daily check kept on the receipt and issue of stores, a periodical stock-taking is necessary for a number of reasons.

The most important object of stock-taking is the ascertaining of the actual value as distinguished from the book value of the stock in hand. However strict the control of the incoming and outgoing stores, it is always found upon stock-taking that there is some difference due to bad handling and inaccurate recording.

Any such discrepancies must be investigated; a reasonable allowance should, however, be made for normal wastage such as evaporation and breakages. Articles which are in poor condition should be listed and, if fit for consumption, some value should be placed on them. Once the stock has been taken and the discrepancies investigated, the stock records should be adjusted to show the actual quantity of each item.

Whilst the valuation of most items of stock presents little difficulty, articles which have been partly converted into dishes, meat for example, may require the stock-taker's particular attention. It is usual, in such cases, to ' gross-up ' the item concerned in order to arrive at its raw weight, and take that grossed-up figure as a basis. The percentage cooking-loss varies from one kind of meat to another and, as a result, an accurate valuation of such items requires a certain amount of experience.

It is usual in most establishments to take stock monthly and, it is considered, that stock-taking at any longer intervals should be avoided. In order to facilitate the actual stock-taking and the valuation of the stock, suitably ruled stock-sheets should be prepared (see page 20).

A SIMPLE SYSTEM FOR THE STORES

We have already mentioned the two alternatives, bin cards and stock cards. It is considered that of the two most medium-sized establishments would find loose-leaf stock books the more convenient. Bin cards are usually more difficult to maintain because they are less easily accessible, being attached to the bins, racks, etc., in different parts of the stores.

Another advantage of stock cards over bin cards is that their maintenance facilitates re-ordering. They are all kept in the same binder or cabinet and, in such circumstances, the actual stock of any one item may be ascertained much more easily.

Incoming Stores On delivery the goods must be checked for quantity and quality. When the storekeeper has satisfied

BLANK CATERING CO., LTD.
STOCK SHEET No.

Date: ....19............

ARTICLE	QUANTITY IN STOCK	UNIT PRICE	£	p	ARTICLE	QUANTITY IN STOCK	UNIT PRICE	£	p

Article ....

Minimum Stock ....
Standard Order ....

DATE	RECEIPTS	ISSUES	BALANCE	DATE	RECEIPTS	ISSUES	BALANCE

STOCK CARD - LARGE SIZE

Article		Minimum Stock	
DATE	RECEIPTS	ISSUES	BALANCE

STOCK CARD - SMALL SIZE; SUITABLE FOR SLOW-MOVING ITEMS

ARTICLE..
MINIMUM STOCK............................... BIN No..................

DATE	RECEIVED	ISSUED	BALANCE

BIN CARD

Blank Catering Co. Ltd.
STORES REQUISITION

Date: ....

Dept.: ....

No.: ....

QUANTITY	UNIT PRICE	£	p

Signed ....

himself that the goods are as ordered, he enters the quantities in the appropriate stock cards (see pages 21 & 22).

Issues All requisitioning departments have to be issued with internal order forms (stores requisitions). The storekeeper's duty is then to see that nothing leaves his department except against a written, properly authorised stores requisition. The order forms should preferably be numbered for reference and filing purposes (see page 23).

Where it is desired to analyse the consumption of stores by departments, the order forms should be easily distinguishable. For instance, different-coloured order forms for different departments could be used. At the end of the day or, in fact, whenever convenient the quantities as per requisitions are entered on the individual stock cards.

In some establishments it may be found that the entering up of stock cards from individual stores requisitions necessitates a continual replacement of stock cards. In order to reduce the turnover of stock cards, however, it is possible to introduce a Weekly Issues Book (see page 25). The object of this book is to summarize the weekly issues to enable a total for each article to be transferred to the respective stock card. An important advantage of the Weekly Issues Book is that it enables the caterer to find the total consumption of non-perishables at the end of each week.

Advantages Some of the advantages even of a simple system for the stores will by now be apparent. There is no doubt that its most important advantage is the provision of cost data.

By analysing the issues at the end of a week—or any period for that matter—we can find the exact consumption of stores for different departments and for the whole business. It is as well to remember that in the absence of a system of stores accounting it is only possible to find the total consumption on stock-taking.

WEEKLY ISSUES BOOK

| Article | Unit Price | ISSUES | | | | | | | Total Issues | Total Value |
		Sunday	Monday	Tuesday	Wednesday	Thursday	Friday	Saturday		£ p

Again, by analysing the issues it is possible to relate consumption to sales and in this way exercise a great deal of control over current expenditure.

In addition to facilitating the control of expenditure a system of stores accounting helps in the purchase of stores. If the stock cards are well kept it is possible to ascertain, within a matter of minutes, the stock of a large number of items without the necessity of referring to the actual stock.

Perishables The above notes do not apply to certain provisions such as fresh meat, fresh fish, milk, cream, etc. These are not kept in the stores but are transferred direct to the kitchen. A suitable method of controlling these items is to maintain a Weekly Perishables Book (see pages 27 & 28) and, at the end of each week relate the consumption of each major item of food to the sales for that week.

FOOD COST CONTROL

Buying In practice the control of food cost must start at the beginning of the full cycle of operations—the purchase of provisions. Skilful buying is quite an art and the proper discharge of this function may result in considerable economies to the establishment.

Effective purchasing involves three basic elements:
(1) Price
(2) Quality
(3) Specification

DATE	SUPPLIER	Inv. No.	TOTAL	MEAT	POULTRY	FISH	BACON & SAUSAGES	MILK & CREAM	FRUIT	Vegetables	SUNDRIES

WEEKLY PERISHABLES BOOK

Date	Supplier	INV. NO.	TOTAL £ p	MEAT			POULTRY			FISH			DAIRY			FRUIT			VEG'BLES		
				QT	£	P.	QT	£	P	QT	£	P	QT	£	P	QT	£	P	QT	£	P

WEEKLY PERISHABLES BOOK

AN ALTERNATIVE RULING

The first element needs little comment. Prices do vary from one supplier to another and the skilful buyer will, other things being equal, try to buy in the cheapest market. The quality of the provisions purchased is at least as important as the price, but it is infinitely more difficult to assess. The ordering of supplies over the telephone is hardly the same thing as buying, for although the price may be known, the quality cannot be assessed in a number of cases except by inspection.

The third element has a more direct bearing on the costs. When buying it is essential to specify the exact weight or size required. If it is known that 3lb. chickens are best suited for a particular purpose, 3lb. birds should be insisted upon. If somewhat heavier chickens were accepted the chef would most probably get the same number of portions out of each, and the excess weight would then represent an unplanned and undesirable increase in food cost, and hence a loss of profit.

The above is only an illustration of the problem which applies to a whole range of items. When supplies are according to specification the cost per portion, and therefore the Kitchen Profit, can be controlled much more easily.

A recent development in this area are *purchase specifications*, which are now widely used in larger hotel and catering organisations. A purchase specification is a precise description of the quality, size and weight of a particular item of food. It is something that is peculiar to a given establishment as, it will be appreciated, the requirements of different establishments may vary quite considerably. The main objectives of purchase specifications are: to inform the suppliers of the exact requirements of the caterer, to establish a purchasing standard and finally to facilitate the control of the quality of incoming goods. Purchase specifications should be available in goods received department; otherwise their object will only be partly fulfilled.

Next, the method of cooking must be considered. During the past decade or two a number of tests have been carried out both in this country and in the U.S.A. As a result we now possess some data regarding such matters as the smoking points of different frying media, the effects of cooking on the shrinkage of meat, the percentage bone loss on different kinds of meat and poultry. We know, for example, that low temperature cooking is in most cases preferable for two main reasons : it results in less shrinkage and secures some economy in fuel consumption.

The fact is that, little as we know about these matters, the fragmentary information we possess is only occasionally utilized by most caterers. Far too little attention is being paid to these matters except perhaps by some large-scale caterers, who are beginning to adopt a scientific approach to the preparation and service of food.

PORTION CONTROL   All caterers have to face the problem of relating the food value given to the customer to the price charged. Now if portions are too generous the caterer will, in all probability, find that his profits are too small; if portions are too small it is more than likely that his customers will turn to his competitors.

The size of the portion must be determined by the management by reference to a number of factors :

(1) The decision will depend on the type of customer— office workers need smaller portions than manual workers.
(2) The portion and its price must be compatible with the customer's spending power. We may add at this stage that the price is only indirectly related to the size of the portion. It is clear that the customer pays not only for the actual food but also for its preparation and service.
(3) Finally the portions must be such as to allow the establishment to earn a satisfactory margin of profit.

These, briefly, are the main considerations by which the management will be guided in determining the size of portions. Once these decisions have been made :

(a) the staff must be informed of the policy,

(b) facilities must be provided conducive to the execution of such policy, for example, proper equipment such as the right capacity ladles, servers, measures,

(c) the staff must be properly supervised to ensure that the policy is adhered to.

The term portion control is often misunderstood and it would be useful for us to explain its meaning at this stage.

Portion control means the determination of the size— whether in terms of weight, volume or otherwise—of each item of food sold to the customer and the adoption of such measures as may be necessary to carry these standards into effect. The practice of portion control does not, in any way, indicate the policy of the management regarding the *size* of portions as such; that is to say portion control means neither large nor small portions—it simply means that portions are standardized. Needless to say portion control can be applied in every type of establishment irrespective of the food value given to the customer.

Standard Recipes. Recipes of various kinds have been in use for generations, and it is essential to distinguish between what is now known as basic recipes and standard recipes. A basic recipe is one which gives general guidance on the preparation of an item of food and is not intended for any particular establishment or type of customer. The recipes found in the majority of cookery books are basic recipes.

A standard recipe is one which is specially written for use in a particular establishment and one which, therefore, pays particular attention to the requirements of its customers. Typically, a standard recipe will list the ingredients, and their quantities; explain in a logical sequence the method of preparation and indicate important factors such as the size/weight of a portion, cost per portion; in some forms of catering the nutritional value of the dish would also be given. It will be readily appreciated that standard recipes offer a number of advantages. They control the ingredients used; they ensure a consistent product for the customer and, finally, they assist the kitchen crew in the preparation of meals.

Service   It is one thing to know exactly the size of each portion to be served and quite another to make sure that correct portions are, in fact, served to the customers. It is, therefore, necessary to institute a system of requisitioning food from the kitchen. We know that in the majority of well-managed hotels, restaurants and other catering establishments such systems are, in fact, in operation. Briefly, whatever applies between the stores and the kitchen equally applies as between the kitchen and the dining-room.

There are of course numerous other problems that demand the caterer's continual attention, for example, how to maintain the food at the correct temperature—a temperature, that is to say, that will keep the food warm enough to be palatable without causing excessive shrinkage or evaporation.

To sum up, the only way to achieve a high degree of efficiency in terms of food cost is continual experimenting, the making of tests, and an adventurous and imaginative approach to the full cycle of catering operations.

METHODS OF FOOD COST CONTROL

The main object of food cost control is to secure the maximum kitchen profit and thus, indirectly, net profit. There are three further methods of controlling the expenditure on food:

(a) Controlling the physical quantity of each main item of food used.

(b) Analysing total food cost into a number of groups such as meat, fish, etc., and thus controlling its percentage composition.

(c) Relating the cost to the sales and, in this way controlling the Kitchen Profit.

THE QUANTITY APPROACH Under this method an attempt is made to compare the consumption of food, in physical terms, with the sale thereof. Now this method in itself is quite inadequate as an instrument of control. A serious objection to this method is that it attempts to control *quantities* rather than costs. The food cost of any one portion depends on two factors :

(a) the quantities of ingredients used, and

(b) the price of each ingredient.

It is obvious that even if correct quantities are used the Kitchen Profit may be quite unsatisfactory as a result of high prices.

In spite of the foregoing criticism quantity control may in certain circumstances be resorted to as an instrument of control. For instance, we can get some idea of whether or not the consumption of tea and coffee is reasonable by comparing the consumption with the number of teas and coffees sold. Again we may divide the total weight of meat consumed in any one period by the number of meals served and, in this way, estimate if the consumption is reasonable; an average of, say, $\frac{1}{2}$ kg. would naturally call for a detailed investigation. These are only one or two illustrations of the uses of quantity control. It will be appreciated that this method can only be applied to some commodities and, for that reason, cannot be exclusively relied upon as a method of control.

FOOD COST ANALYSIS Under the second method which, by the way, is widely used in the Hotel and Catering Industry, we analyse the weekly or monthly expenditure on food into a number of groups such as meat, poultry, fish, vegetables, groceries, etc. Obviously the larger the number of groups the more effective the method. It is considered, however, that most medium-sized hotels and restaurants would not need more than 10-12 groups.

Having analysed the total expenditure on food we then express each group as a percentage of either :

(a) total food cost or, as is more usual,
(b) total sales.

This second method rests on the assumption that there is a definite relationship between any one group and total food cost or total sales. A caterer might know, for instance, that his average expenditure on meat and poultry amounts to $17 \cdot 5$ per cent of his revenue. If at the end of a certain period he found that this percentage had increased to, say, $19 \cdot 8$ per cent of sales he would have to investigate the reasons for the increase which might be due to any one or a combination of the following :

(a) increased prices charged by suppliers,
(b) inferior quality resulting in excessive wastage,
(c) bad handling and faulty preparation,
(d) petty pilfering or other leakages in the system,
(e) too low selling prices.

The food cost analysis method is certainly an effective check. It is fairly simple and can be operated at a minimum cost. It has, however, some limitations.

Successful menu planning must be conditioned by seasonal price fluctuations and, because of the change in the composition of the menu, there are often substantial variations in the cost of the different groups. Again as a result of periodical price changes it is to some extent misleading to compare the cost of a group of commodities in July with that of June even in the absence of any changes in the composition of the menu. It is, subject to any price changes, more logical to compare the cost of a group in June of the current year, with the corresponding cost in June the previous year.

These are briefly some of the objections to the second method. The analysis of the percentage composition of total food cost should preferably be weekly rather than monthly. If there is an unjustifiable increase in the cost of any group it is obviously in the caterer's interest to take the necessary remedial action as soon as possible and, for that reason, a monthly analysis is always less effective than a weekly analysis.

Where there is no system of stores accounting, a weekly analysis of purchases and consumption is difficult; it is even more difficult where stock is taken at monthly intervals. On the other hand where there is a system of food requisitioning by means of written stores requisitions, ascertaining the weekly food cost or its analysis presents little difficulty.

Perishables Those provisions which are transferred direct to the kitchen, for example, fresh meat, fresh fish, milk, etc., would not be subject to any system of food requisitioning. Yet if we are to analyse the total cost of food, these items must clearly be taken into account. The total weekly or monthly cost of these provisions and the percentages may be worked out if a Weekly Perishables Book is kept (see pages 27 & 28). The consumption for any one period would be calculated as follows :

Opening Stock + Provisions Received
— Closing Stock = Consumption

If it is desirable to know the quantities consumed in addition to the values, the data will be available if quantity columns are provided (see page 28).

KITCHEN PROFIT CONTROL   The third method of food cost control is, no doubt, the best method we have at our disposal. It is, however, more complicated and more costly to operate, and cannot, for that reason, be adopted except by large catering units.

Briefly, the object of this method is to analyse both total food cost and total receipts and control the percentage Kitchen Profit on each major item of food, or sub-department of the kitchen, separately.

Let us now assume that the food sold by an establishment is, for control purposes, divided into six groups, A, B, C, D, E and F. In such circumstances each section would have to requisition its own food from the stores and the food cost of each section would thus be known. In order to ascertain the Kitchen Profit achieved by each section the sales would have to be analysed in accordance with the analysis of food consumed.

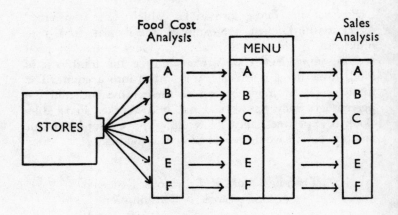

It will be appreciated that, in this method, food cost analysis must correspond with sales analysis; otherwise the calculation of the respective percentages of Kitchen Profit would be impossible. Whereas the cost of food is analysed on the basis of stores requisitions, sales analysis is usually carried out on the basis of waiters' checks.

The percentage Kitchen Profit will vary from one group to another quite considerably. It would be most unwise to try to secure a uniform percentage of profit on all items sold. Thus the Kitchen Profit on soups will probably be higher than the profit on fish; coffees will invariably show a smaller percentage than teas but, in all probability, a higher percentage than poultry.

CONCLUSIONS

We have now outlined the most common clerical procedures which must be adopted if a costing system is to work satisfactorily. We have also described the most common methods of food cost control and some of the major problems that always have to be faced.

The reader will, no doubt, agree that a system of material costing is an important tool in the hands of the management. But, the fact remains, the results produced by any system largely depend on its intelligent application. Let us, therefore, conclude this chapter with a few words of warning.

The Human Factor First it must be understood that costing will not produce the desired results unless it takes the human factor into account. The system must be simple in order to be understood by those who are responsible for its operation. It should, as far as possible, be built up round the existing structure of organization. Finally, in order to function smoothly, it must be based on a superstructure of inter-departmental goodwill and co-operation.

A realistic approach to material costing must, in addition, take the following factors into account:

1. Correct Buying The following rules should be observed when buying provisions:

(a) In order to facilitate control it is desirable to buy such food where it is comparatively easy to relate the food cost per portion to the selling price.

(b) It is imperative to remember that correct buying is buying on the basis of yield per portion rather than price; what matters is the cost per portion on the plate rather than the price per lb. paid to the supplier.

(c) Efficient buying must necessarily be conditioned by the seasonal price fluctuations of the provisions used. The caterer's aim should be to take advantage of such price fluctuations without, if possible, allowing them to be reflected in the prices charged. For the purposes of both costing and price-fixing an average price for each item of food should be calculated.

2. Menu-planning Menu-planning is frequently neglected, no doubt because its importance is not always fully appreciated. The menu should be planned at least a week in advance in all small and medium-sized establishments. A menu with a few simple but well prepared dishes is certainly preferable to one which looks impressive but, owing to lack of qualified staff, results in unpalatable food.

When planning the menu the following must be taken into consideration:

(a) The estimated volume of sales.
(b) The type of customer.
(c) The state of the market.
(d) The utilization of 'left-overs.'

An important condition of successful menu-planning is that nothing should be placed on the menu unless the item

concerned has been pre-costed. To facilitate the costing of
the different items offered to the customer, a Portion Costing Sheet (see page 40) may be used. The main advantage
of this simple form is that it helps the caterer to control his
profit margins. In larger organizations standard recipes
should be produced and adhered to.

3. Strict Control Owing to the complexity of catering
operations it is frequently found that no one single method
of control is adequate to secure the best results; a single line
of attack will just not do. A comprehensive and multilineal
approach to the problem is therefore essential. This should
take the form of spot-checks on :
(a) Incoming goods.
(b) Prices paid to suppliers and discounts received.
(c) Consumption of food (see above, *Methods of Food Cost
Control*).
(d) Utilization of ' left-overs.'
(e) Menu prices.

An occasional spot-check is usually a matter of minutes
and the time thus spent is, more often than not, worthwhile.

PORTION COSTING SHEET

Date: .... Checked by: ....

DISH		1		2		3		4		5		6	
		£	p	£	p	£	p	£	p	£	p	£	p
BUT-CHER													
FISH													
DAIRY													
GREEN GR'CER													
STORES													
TOTAL													
No of portions													
Cost per portion													

CHAPTER FOUR

LABOUR

Our task now is to devote some attention to the second element of cost—labour. It is hardly possible to over-emphasize how important it is to control the total expenditure falling under this heading. Wage costs have tended to rise for a long time and, at present, the expenditure on labour represents about 25 per cent of net sales in the average catering business.

RECORDS

Where there is a costing system in operation certain records must be kept. Such records are necessary for a number of purposes; first, for the compilation of the pay-roll at the end of each week, for the analysis of labour costs as between different departments, and for control purposes. Secondly there must be some system of time recording. In some large hotels there are automatic time-recording clocks, and there is no doubt that automatic time-recording is of great assistance as an instrument of expense control. In the smaller establishment it is useful to keep a Staff Time Book for this purpose (see page 42).

INCLUSIVE COST OF LABOUR

The total cost of labour consists of a number of distinct items all of which, from the costing point of view, have to

TIME SHEET

Employee's Name..........................

Department..........................

Week Commencing..........................

Normal Working Hours..........................(per week)

	SUNDAY			MONDAY			TUESDAY			WEDNESDAY			THURSDAY			FRIDAY			SATURDAY			WEEKLY TOTALS
	From	To	Hrs.	From	To	Hrs.	From	To	Hrs.	From	To	Hrs.	From	To	Hrs.	From	To	Hrs.	From	To	Hrs.	
Normal Time																						
"																						
Total Normal Time																							
Overtime																							
Daily Totals																							

Signed..........................   Checked..........................

RECORD CARD

Surname................................ Other Names...............................

Date of Birth.................... Place of Birth.................... Married/Single

Occupation.......................... Department....................

Private Address..

Date Commenced........................ Wages/Salary....................

Date Left.................... Reason....................

Other Particulars..

....

....

be considered as labour. The inclusive cost of labour usually consists of :

(a) The actual gross wages and salaries paid.

(b) Employer's social security contributions.

(c) Staff meals. The cost of feeding the staff cannot logically be regarded as part of the food cost. It is usual to make a certain allowance for staff feeding, for example, 25p per full-time employee per day which, for costing purposes, is added to the cost of labour.

(d) Cost of replacing labour. In the Hotel and Catering Industry the rate of labour-turnover is certainly higher than the average for the national economy. Efficient management, with all its implications, such as proper lighting and ventilation, well-planned working hours, is an important factor in limiting the rate of labour-turnover. Apart from involving the establishment in some expense of replacement, a high rate of turnover is detrimental to the morale of the staff. Moreover, new workers have to be trained and they need more supervision in the initial period when, it is well to note, their output is low.

CONTROL OF LABOUR COSTS

We mentioned in an earlier chapter (see page 10) that it would be impracticable in this industry to apportion the total cost of labour to the individual items of food sold and that, as a result, the only course open to most caterers is to control the total cost of labour whilst controlling the Kitchen Profit on the individual items of food.

How can we control the inclusive cost of labour as a percentage of net sales? Is it always possible to limit the cost of labour to a definite percentage of sales and maintain it at that level?

In the seasonal type of business most of the labour force would only be employed during the season, say, from April to September, and in such circumstances—particularly where part-time labour is available—the cost of labour will correspond to a great extent to the volume of business done. However, in order to achieve a high degree of adjustment of wage costs to sales a certain amount of planning is imperative, and here even a simple system of costing will prove of great value.

Where past records are available it is possible to analyse the sales for the past two or three years on a time basis. The analysis will certainly disclose a definite trend of sales over the calendar year and thus indicate the size of the labour force necessary each month. Naturally, in addition to the data extracted from past records other factors would have to be taken into account, for example, current developments and trends in the locality, and general business prospects.

In the non-seasonal type of business the position is somewhat different. In many establishments a fixed number of staff have to be kept irrespective of the periodical fluctuations in the volume of sales. When that is so, it is by no means an easy task to maintain the cost of labour as a fixed percentage of sales. The problem must, unfortunately, be faced and indeed accepted as a challenge; the caterer must make an effort to keep the wages down to the minimum and yet make sure that his staff, in numerical terms, are sufficient for the expected standard of service.

Let us now illustrate, by means of a simple example, the relationship between sales and labour costs.

	June	July	Aug.	Sep.
Sales	£1,000	£1,200	£1,300	£800
Labour ...	250	250	250	250
Labour % of Sales ...	25%	20·8%	19·2%	31·2%

Now if the establishment is working at a moderate percentage of profit, failure to control wage costs may well produce highly unsatisfactory results. The fixity of wage costs is clearly one of those problems which deserve the caterer's particular attention.

It will be appreciated that the volume of sales is governed by many factors some of which are outside the management's control. The cost of labour, on the other hand, although fairly stable may nevertheless be controlled to some extent and varied as a matter of conscious policy.

We have already mentioned the forecasting of labour requirements on the basis of past sales and the problems created by a high rate of labour-turnover. There are a number of methods of reducing the cost of labour.

The introduction of labour-saving devices is often an economical proposition, although the extent to which labour can be replaced by machinery depends primarily on the size of the establishment. Even in small hotels and restaurants, however, there is some scope for the introduction of new machinery and better equipment. The initial cost is often quite high but, in the long run, the expense is a good investment. In many hotels every fourth meal is an employee meal—a fact so often overlooked by caterers considering the purchase of labour-saving machinery. Perhaps the best method of controlling wage costs in large establishments is to have a labour budget (see chapter 8). This will show where labour costs are out of line and thus enable the management to take the necessary remedial action.

CHAPTER FIVE

OVERHEADS

The control of the overheads is as important as the control of labour costs. In most catering establishments the cost of the overheads represents about 20 per cent of the takings; this percentage is only an average and there are quite considerable differences in this respect within the industry.

Overheads, just as labour costs, vary little with the volume of business and a reduction in the size of this expense is usually difficult to achieve. Every meal sold by the caterer carries a certain amount of overheads and, given the price, a decrease in the total cost of overheads produces a higher percentage of profit.

Overheads may be defined as all items of expense other than those falling under the heading of materials (food costs) or labour costs.

CONTROL OF OVERHEADS

In practice some expenses are much more difficult to control than others. Depreciation, for example, is one of those items of expense the control of which presents some difficulty.

REF.	DATE OF PURCHASE	DESCRIPTION	SUPPLIER	COST £	COST p	Depreciation %	REMARKS

EQUIPMENT REGISTER

Once an asset (for example, electric oven, potato-peeler) has been purchased the annual cost of depreciation becomes an unavoidable, continuous expense. Other expenses, for example, printing, stationery, postage can be controlled more easily and where necessary, varied as a matter of deliberate policy.

It will be convenient now to divide expenditure into two groups :

(a) Capital Expenditure—this may be defined as expenditure which results in the acquisition of fixed assets, for example, electric mixing machines, dish-washing machines, cutlery, furniture, fittings.

(b) Revenue Expenditure—this may be defined as all expenditure (other than that on provisions) which does not result in the acquisition of fixed assets, for example, rent, rates, insurance, postage, printing, etc.

CONTROL OF CAPITAL EXPENDITURE

The reader will realize that capital expenditure as such is not a part of overheads. The acquisition of an asset, however, entails a continuous expense over a period of years. As the value of an asset diminishes with the passage of time a proportion of its original cost must be deducted and charged against current profits. This diminution in the value of an asset is known as depreciation.

There are three main methods of depreciation :

1. The Straight-Line Method   Under this method the original cost of the asset, less any scrap value, is divided by the estimated life of the asset, thus :

Original Cost of Asset   ...   £120
Less Scrap Value (say)   ...   10

Amount to be written off   ...   £110
If estimated Life of Asset   10 years
Then Depreciation at a fixed rate of £ 11 per annum.

The straight-line method of depreciation is simple in application and very much used in all branches of the hotel and catering industry.

2. *The Reducing Balance Method*   Under this method a fixed percentage is written off each year, calculated on the value of the asset at the beginning of the year. The amount to be written off diminishes with the value of the asset.

Example:
Original Cost of Asset   £120·00
Less Scrap Value (say)   10·00

Amount to be written off   110·00
Less 10% Depreciation—1st year   11·00

Book Value at the end of the 1st year   99·00
Less 10% Depreciation—2nd year   9·90

Book Value at the end of the 2nd year   89·10
Less 10% Depreciation—3rd year   8·91

Book Value at the end of the 3rd year   £80·19., etc.

The cost of an asset is made up of depreciation and repairs, and both have to be charged against current profits. Whilst the amount of depreciation under this method becomes progressively less, the cost of repairs is, as a rule, more at the end than at the beginning of the life of the asset. As a result the charge against the profits of the establishment is more or less constant.

3. Revaluation Method It would be impracticable to work out the individual amounts of depreciation on small items of equipment such as cutlery, corkscrews, ice-cream servers, plate and linen. Such equipment is best depreciated by the revaluation method. A periodical inventory is made and the difference between the value of such equipment at the beginning of the period and at the end of the period is written off as depreciation.

The control of overheads, as far as capital expenditure is concerned, presents a number of problems. When an asset is purchased in the first place the expenditure must be viewed as a kind of investment. The choice of the asset will normally be conditioned by a number of factors such as its price, the estimated life of the asset, and above all, its suitability for the purpose for which it is required. In the case of heavy equipment .such as pastry-ovens, boilers, potato-peelers, a regular inspection is necessary to ensure that the equipment is, at all times, in good working condition.

In order to exercise the requisite degree of control over the establishment's fixed assets, and to facilitate the production of cost data, it is advised that a periodical (at least annual) inventory be undertaken. It is useful to keep a register for the main items of equipment showing the original cost, the percentage depreciation and other relevant information (see page 48).

CONTROL OF REVENUE EXPENDITURE

The control of revenue expenditure is in some respects less difficult than the control of capital expenditure. Most revenue expenses take the form of frequent payments, for example, printing, stationery, cleaning materials, postage, and provided a constant check is being kept they will not increase out of proportion to the volume of sales.

There is, however, another group of items, for example, rent, rates, insurances, licences—comprising expenditure which, at least in the short run, is unavoidable and fixed. In such cases the only advice that can be given is that each long-term commitment should be carefully considered before the final decision is made; wherever possible one should rely on the advice of an expert, particularly when renting or buying premises.

The most effective method of control in the case of the overheads is constant analysis. For this purpose it is possible to obtain most of the information from the financial records. Thus, the expenditure on rent, rates, postage, etc., may be easily obtained from the nominal or trading ledger. When the expense is paid periodically, such as gas and electricity, it is possible to read the meters weekly or monthly and calculate the cost with a great degree of accuracy.

In order to bring to light an undesirable increase in any one expense it is essential to check periodically the percentage composition of the total overhead expenditure. This may be done in two different ways : by expressing each item of expense as a percentage of either (a) total overheads, or (b) total sales (see page 53).

Comparative percentages for previous trading periods are, of course, very helpful.

OVERHEADS COST ANALYSIS SHEET
Percentages on Total Overheads

	JANUARY		FEBRUARY		MARCH		APRIL		MAY		JUNE	
	THIS YEAR	LAST YEAR	THIS YEAR	LAST YEAR	THIS YEAR	LAST YEAR	THIS YEAR	LAST YEAR	THIS YEAR	LAST YEAR	THIS YEAR	LAST YEAR
Rent and Rates												
Heat, Light, Power												
Repairs, Maintenance												
Depreciation												
Printing, Stationery												
Postage, Telephone												
Licences, Insurance												
Legal, Bank Charges												
Other Expenses												
TOTAL	100%	100%	100%	100%	100%	100%	100%	100%	100%	100%	100%	100%

CHAPTER SIX

PROFIT

We have now reached the stage when we can usefully devote some attention to the nature and significance of profit.

It is often said that ' profit is the driving force of enterprise '—a general assumption frequently made to facilitate the explanation of certain economic decisions and a proposition which, although substantially valid, merits a more detailed examination.

There is no doubt that the size of the Net Profit earned by the caterer is of the greatest importance; the acquisition of profit is most certainly his major object. We should however be on our guard not to oversimplify the complexity of business behaviour, lest we should fall into the trap of presuming the caterer—or any business man for that matter—to think solely in terms of profit. That type of behaviour would, in fact, be the exception rather than the rule.

We know that it is not only the ' desire to maximize profits ' that stimulates business activity, and that the business man is also guided by other considerations such as his desire for independence, or the pride he takes in his business.

When we turn from the individual caterer to the hotel and catering industry we see that here the problem is at least as complicated. Apart from commercial catering—that part of the industry which is run for profit—a fair proportion of catering is undertaken on a ' non-profit basis.' Under this heading we have most industrial canteens, hospital catering and numerous forms of institutional catering.

In conclusion it may be said that, although the purpose of catering cannot be explained in terms of any one single object, from the individual caterer's point of view the profit is, in fact, of the greatest importance. Further, the size of the Net Profit earned is indicative of the relative success of a business, and it is only by reference to the profit gained by an establishment that we can determine whether or not it is successful. There is, unfortunately, no other yard-stick of success.

HOW MUCH NET PROFIT?

The question is often asked ' how much profit should one aim at in catering?' The answer to this question is by no means easy. To say that, as the caterer's main object is profit, he should try to make as much as he possibly can, would be rather naïve and, for practical purposes, of little value.

The hotel and catering industry consists of a large number of establishments of a diverse nature and, for that reason, any generalizations would be both unwise and dangerous. There are however certain criteria which are helpful in determining the ' normal ' profit in any one particular case.

Firstly, we have the element of risk. The greater the degree of risk involved the greater, consequently, should be the size of the intended profit. Thus an old-established business, relying on regular all-year-round custom, will be satisfied with a smaller margin of profit than one subject to severe fluctuations in its volume of business.

Secondly, we know that profit margins in catering are by no means excessive. The evidence at our disposal tends to indicate that the majority of catering businesses operate on Net Profit margins ranging from 9 to 15 per cent of sales.

Finally, let it be remembered that profit consists of two distinct elements :

(a) the return on the capital invested,
(b) the wages of management.

Bearing that in mind we have to conclude that, if an establishment is to be considered a success, the Net Profit earned must give a sufficient return on the capital invested; in the case of a personally-managed establishment, the Net Profit must also be ample to remunerate the proprietor for his services.

PROFIT AS A YARDSTICK OF SUCCESS

As we said in an earlier chapter, it is usual in catering to express both costs and profits as percentages of sales. This, experience shows, is a convenient and simple method of expressing the relationship between costs and profits on the one hand and sales on the other.

Whilst there is no reason at all to advocate a discontinuance of this procedure, it seems that it has resulted in a certain misapprehension : many caterers appear to be under the impression that it is possible to use the percentage of Net Profit on sales as a yardstick of profitability. This is a misconception.

The percentage of Net Profit on sales is only indicative of the relative operating efficiency of an establishment at two different trading periods. It stands in no direct relationship to the overall profitability of the business. In order to determine whether or not an establishment is profitable we have to express the Net Profit earned as a percentage of the capital invested. In the case of a personally-managed establishment a due allowance has to be made for the owner's services.

It is sometimes alleged that there is no point in expressing the Net Profit as a percentage of the capital invested because, it is said, the assets disclosed by the balance sheet are not shown at their true value. True, they are not—but that does not affect the validity of our argument. It has to be realized that the balance sheet must conform to certain legal requirements (for example, those of the Companies Acts of 1948 and 1967). Further, the actual presentation of this document is determined, to a considerable extent, by current accounting practice.

It is, as a result, of little consequence that the figures disclosed in the balance sheet do not always represent true economic values, so long as those who make use of it are fully aware of the fact. What matters is that there is in each business a certain amount of capital which has a definite realisable value.

Consider now the following hypothetical example:

	RESTAURANT A			RESTAURANT B		
Capital invested in the business		£28,000			£16,000	
Net Sales		£20,000	100%		£20,000	100%
Less Food Cost	8,200	41%		8,200	41%	
Wages	5,200	26%		5,200	26%	
Overheads	3,800	19%	17,200	3,800	19%	17,200
			86%			86%
Profit on Sales		2,800	14%		2,800	14%
Less Reward for Proprietor's Services		800	4%		800	4%
Net Profit on Sales		£2,000	10%		£2,000	10%
NET PROFIT ON CAPITAL INVESTED			7.1%			12.5%

If we disregarded the capital invested in the two restaurants, the profits expressed as percentages of sales would suggest that both restaurants are equally profitable and that both are earning reasonably good profits. In fact Restaurant A does not produce an adequate return on the capital invested, whilst Restaurant B shows a reasonable profit.

PROFIT AND THE VOLUME OF BUSINESS

We saw in an earlier chapter that the total cost of any one dish consists of three basic elements: materials (food cost), labour and overheads. For certain purposes, however, it is convenient to divide the total cost into:

(a) *Fixed Costs*—costs which do not vary directly with the volume of business, for example rent, rates, insurances, licences (also, in a non-seasonal establishment, wages).

(b) *Variable Costs*—costs which vary directly with the volume of business, such as food cost.

By definition, therefore, an increase in the volume of business will result in a proportional increase in the variable charges, the fixed charges being constant. Similarly, a decrease in the volume of business will result in a corresponding decrease in the variable charges, the fixed charges being again constant. It follows, therefore, that an increase in the amount of trade done will result in a less than proportionate increase in the total cost and a larger net profit and *vice versa*.

It is mainly because of the fixity of the wages and overheads that it is essential for each caterer to secure an adequate volume of business in order to secure a satisfactory margin of Net Profit.

The following table indicates the influence of the volume of business on the profitability of an establishment.

NUMBER OF CUSTOMERS PER WEEK	WEEKLY SALES IF AVERAGE PRICE OF MEAL=40p.	SALES PER ANNUM	KITCHEN PROFIT IF FOOD COST 40 PER CENT.	LESS— ASSUMED FIXED COSTs (WAGES AND OVERHEADS)	NET PROFIT PER ANNUM	NET PROFIT— PERCENTAGE OF SALES	NET PROFIT— PERCENTAGE OF (ASSUMED) CAPITAL £15,000
600	£240	£12,480	£7,488	£7,000	£488	3.9%	3.3%
650	£260	£13,520	£8,112	£7,000	£1,112	8.2%	7.4%
700	£280	£14,560	£8,736	£7,000	£1,736	11.9%	11.6%
750	£300	£15,600	£9,360	£7,000	£2,360	15.1%	15.7%
800	£320	£16,640	£9,984	£7,000	£2,984	17.9%	19.9%

BREAK-EVEN CHARTS

As may be seen from the table on page 59 the volume of sales achieved by the catering establishment is one of the most important factors determining its net profit. A useful device which is often used to show the relationship between sales, costs and profits is known as the break-even chart.

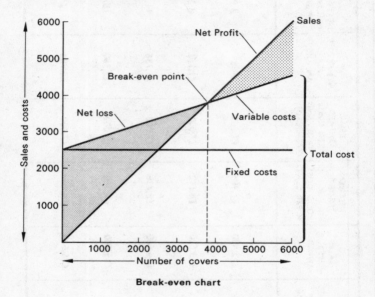

Break-even chart

A break-even chart is constructed by showing along the horizontal axis the level of activity (usually the number of covers). The vertical axis is used to show the costs and sales of the business.

Let us take an example.

Example. A restaurant serves up to 6,000 covers per month, and the average spending power is £1·00. Hence the maximum monthly sales are £6,000. The variable costs of the restaurant amount to one-third of the volume of sales and its fixed costs are £2,500 per month. A break-even chart would be constructed as shown on page 50.

As may be seen from the break-even chart 3,750 customers must be served in order for the restaurant to cover its costs. Only then does it begin to make a profit.

Let us assume that one month only 3,750 covers are served. A summary of the trading account of the restaurant would look something like this:

Sales (3,750 covers @ £1·00)	£3,750
Less variable costs ($\frac{1}{3}$ of sales)	1,250
	2,500
Less fixed costs	2,500
Net Profit/Loss	NIL

CHAPTER SEVEN

PRICE POLICY

IMPORTANCE OF CORRECT PRICING

It is hardly necessary to stress the importance of correct pricing. It is clear that the prices charged, together with the quality of food and service, determine not only the type of customer attracted but also, to a considerable extent, the volume of business.

The effect of the volume of business on profitability has already been shown. It can be seen, therefore, that the greater the volume of business secured by the caterer the smaller the proportion of net sales required to meet the fixed charges and the larger, therefore, the size of his net profit. Hence the importance of the right price policy, hence the influence of correct pricing methods on the profitability of the business.

TRADITIONAL PRICING METHODS

Pricing methods in catering are in some respects similar to those in other industries. We know that there is in each industry a certain rate of profit which the business man regards as ' fair ' or ' normal.' The selling price is fixed by adding to the variable (prime) cost a certain percentage which covers the fixed charges and, at the same time produces this 'fair' or 'normal' rate of profit. That is what, in fact, we see in catering. One ascertains the food cost (variable cost) and adds a certain percentage of Kitchen Profit to fix the selling price.

FIXING THE 'RIGHT PRICE'

Now it is obvious that whilst this 'food cost-plus-Kitchen Profit' method of pricing is both simple and eminently suitable for some purposes, its rigid application would most certainly produce bad results.

Let us assume that we have produced a certain dish and know, from our costing records, that its food cost is 10p. Let us further assume that our total food cost is equal to 40 per cent. of our total takings. If we were to apply our food cost-plus-Kitchen Profit method of pricing rigidly, our selling price would be fixed as follows:

Food Cost	10p =	40%
Add Kitchen Profit	15p =	60%
Selling Price	25p =	100%

Having added 60 per cent. to our food cost, how are we to know that 25p is, in fact, the correct price to charge? Does the mere fact that the sum total of our expenditure on food gives us a certain ratio of food cost to sales mean that the dish should be sold at 25p? It seems that the answer to this second question must be in the negative.

The following are the main factors that would have to be taken into account when fixing the price of any one item :
(a) The first and most important thing to remember is that the food cost-plus-Kitchen Profit method should be used

as a rough guide only. Because it is an overall, historical ratio of total food cost to total sales, it need not be indicative of what price should be charged in any one particular case.

(b) The composition and the presentation of the dish are factors of major importance. If the composition and the external appearance of the dish are such as to suggest that the customer would be willing to pay a higher price than that indicated by the food cost-plus-Kitchen Profit approach, there is no reason why an attempt should not be made to secure a higher percentage of Kitchen Profit. The fact is that the customer is not interested in the caterer's percentages; what matters, from his point of view, is good food and efficient service at a reasonable price.

(c) Further, it has to be realized that, although for want of a better method prices in catering are fixed on the basis of food cost only, the customer does not pay only for the cost of the food provided. In addition to the food, the customer expects a particular standard of service. The price he pays, therefore, must be such as to cover all the three elements of cost and the necessary margin of profit.

As a result, differences in the cost and profit composition of total sales will determine the differences in the gross profit margins aimed at by different caterers.

Consider now the following hypothetical figures for two restaurants :

	RESTAURANT A	RESTAURANT B
Food Cost	33%	46%
Labour	27%	24%
Overheads	30%	20%
Net Profit	10%	10%
Sales	100%	100%

Let us now assume that both restaurants have produced an ' identical ' dish at a food cost of 10p. In order to cover the fixed charges and the Net Profit, Restaurant A would have to price it at about (see below, (d)) 30p, Restaurant B at about 22p. It can be seen, therefore, that the difference in the prices charged by the two restaurants is due to the fact that Restaurant A provides a better type of service, resulting in relatively higher expenditure on wages and overheads.

(d) Finally, experience shows that the prices charged need not all be proportional to the cost of ingredients used; in other words it is possible to secure a higher percentage of Kitchen Profit on some dishes than on others. Thus, the profit on a mixed grill is invariably less than the profit on fried cod and chips. A sardine and cress sandwich will certainly produce more profit than a ham and tomato sandwich. The percentage of profit on teas is always considerably more than the overall percentage on food, etc.

TABLE D'HOTE AND A LA CARTE MENUS

The planning of an *à la carte* menu is, in some ways, easier than the planning of a table d'hôte menu. In the case of the latter the choice offered to the client must of necessity be more restricted, first because of the ever-present danger of over-production and secondly for reasons of cost.

In the case of the *à la carte* menu it is very much easier to give effect to the varying food cost by charging prices which correspond with it. *A la carte* prices are invariably higher than table d'hôte prices. That is so for three main reasons :

(1) The cost of labour is higher because each dish is prepared individually on receipt of the customer's order.

(2) Customers are usually given better food value.

(3) Customers are prepared to pay higher prices because the *à la carte* menu is associated with more choice and better value.

The table d'hôte menu usually attracts a more uniform type of customer which, no doubt, is largely due to the fixed price charged. As a result, the caterer is more able to get to know the requirements of his clients and set his standards accordingly. In this respect an important advantage of the *à la carte* menu is that it aims at a wider market.

CHAPTER EIGHT

BUDGETARY CONTROL

A system of cost accounting which is confined to the ascertainment of past, historical costs will not prove an efficient tool in the hands of the management. Ascertaining past costs may, it is true, produce a great deal of interesting cost information; however, it does little to help control the caterer's future expenditure. It follows, therefore, that an efficient system of costing must be combined with a system of budgetary control.

Budgetary control may be defined as the setting of predetermined or standard costs, their comparison with actual costs and the subsequent investigation of the differences between the intended and the actual results.

Budgeting must not, however, be regarded as an intellectual exercise. The budget must be realistic and related to actual performance. The full cycle of the budget should, logically, follow the plan ·

(1) detailed planning of the system;
(2) setting of objectives for those responsible;
(3) creation of circumstances conducive to the attainment of such objectives;

(4) comparison of actual with intended results;

(5) notification of results to those responsible;

(6) adoption of such corrective measures as may be necessary.

As the chief purpose of budgeting is to control expenditure the budget, if it is to be an effective instrument of control, must be based on the structure of executive responsibility; for it is obvious that no useful purpose would be served by making a manager responsible for something he cannot control. There is another point to remember when the budget is being prepared; it is imperative to consult departmental managers and secure their co-operation and their agreement to the budget estimates.

A comprehensive system of budgeting must cover both expenditure and income.

EXPENDITURE

At the commencement of the financial year it is necessary to prepare an Expense Budget, showing all items of expenditure predetermined in relation to the estimated volume of business. That is by no means an easy task as a given change in the volume of business will never produce a proportionate change in the total cost. Thus a ten per cent increase in the volume of sales may not affect some items of expense at all, for example rent, rates, insurance; other expenses will increase in proportion, such as the cost of materials used (food cost). Finally there is a group of expenses—known as semi-variable costs—which vary in sympathy with but not quite in proportion to the volume of business, for example lighting, heating, cleaning materials, etc.

It is because of the varying effect on different costs of a given change in the sales that it is necessary to estimate the size of each item of expense separately.

DETERMINATION OF COSTS

When determining the annual cost estimates it is convenient to divide the sum total of expenditure into three groups :

1. Fixed Costs Under this heading we find such items as rent, rates, insurance, licences, etc. A characteristic of fixed costs is that the size of each item is fixed and cannot, in the short run, be varied by the management. It is however necessary to investigate most items of fixed costs as even these may vary owing to factors outside the management's control. Thus, although the rateable value of the premises remains constant over a period of time, the exact size of the expense each year will largely depend on the local authority concerned rather than on the management of the establishment. Again there may be periodical increases in the cost of licences, etc. To sum up, the determination of each particular cost is a question of an intelligent analysis of past cost records in the light of current expectations; this, by the way, applies to all the three groups of expenditure.

2. Variable Costs In catering, perhaps the only item of cost that varies in proportion to sales is the food cost. Unlike other industries the cost of labour is fairly stable. The caterer may know from his past records that his food cost is, say, 40 per cent of the sales. If he estimates a ten per cent increase in the volume of business—and still intends to give the customer 40 per cent food value—he must allow for a ten per cent increase in the food cost. In these days of rising prices his estimate should, of course, be adjusted for the estimated increase in the prices paid to suppliers.

3. Semi-Variable Costs Most items of expense are of a semi-variable nature, that is to say, they vary in sympathy with but not quite in proportion to the volume of sales. In order to determine the estimated annual expenditure for each item it is, first of all, necessary to investigate past records. If these have been kept on a uniform basis for the past few years, it will be possible to determine fairly accurately the effect of a given change in the sales on each item of cost.

Once the annual cost estimates have been predetermined, the management should endeavour to maintain actual costs as closely as possible to the predetermined estimates.

THE BUDGET PERIOD

No general rule can be laid down regarding the length of the budget period. The nature and circumstances of each establishment will, however, tend to indicate the most suitable and convenient period.

It would appear that in the case of the majority of medium-sized catering businesses an annual budget will be the most appropriate; seasonal catering establishments would probably find it convenient to have two budgets— an on- and off-season budget.

Having predetermined the annual costs the next step is to produce a Monthly Expense Budget and Weekly Expense Budget. Daily budgets would be impracticable for most medium-sized and small businesses.

From the point of view of the medium-sized business the weekly rather than monthly budget is the most effective instrument of control, as it allows the caterer to review the history of a fairly short financial period and, if necessary, adopt any preventative or corrective measures that may be necessary. A budget covering any longer period is still very useful in that it reveals possible losses due to inefficiencies in the use of materials, labour, etc. It has to be remembered, however, that a monthly budget is insufficient for the purposes of an effective day-to-day control.

WEEKLY AND MONTHLY BUDGETS

The subdivision of the annual estimates into monthly or weekly budgets is a simple process in cases where the establishment enjoys a steady volume of trade all the year round. In such circumstances all that is necessary (with the exception of one or two items of cost) is to divide the annual estimates by twelve or fifty-two, as the case may be. In the case of establishments relying on seasonal trade or otherwise subject to substantial periodic fluctuation in the volume of sales the Expense Budget must be based on the expected volume of business and the individual items of cost adjusted accordingly.

We have now discussed the broad outlines of budgetary control as applied to the establishment's expenditure, and the main advantages of budgeting should by now be apparent. The reader will have observed that the investigation of the differences (variances, in costing terminology) between the estimated and the actual expenditure is most certainly likely to reveal certain inefficiencies and weaknesses and thus enable prompt corrective measures to be taken.

It is clear that, given a good system of budgetary control, the cost of providing service need not be accepted as a fact; it should rather be considered as a variable quantity whose size depends on the policy and quality of management.

SALES BUDGET

The preparation of a Sales Budget is, in one respect, less difficult than the preparation of an Expense Budget. In the case of the latter we have to estimate the size of each item of expense and that, in itself, is a lengthy process.

The Sales Budget essentially consists of one estimate, namely the total volume of business—although it is useful, in certain establishments, to estimate separately the volume of sales for each section of the business. Thus for an unlicensed restaurant only one figure need be estimated—the total of food sales. In a large licensed hotel it would be necessary to estimate a number of figures separately, namely the sales of food, wines and spirits, banqueting sales, sundry sales such as cigarettes, the rate of occupancy, etc.

The determination of the Sales Budget figures is, of course, mainly a question of sound judgment based on facts and figures relating to the establishment.

In each case the Sales Budget will have to be based on :
(a) The internal records of the establishment.
(b) Published information relating to the catering industry and to business conditions in general.

The first step in the preparation of a Sales Budget is to ascertain the trend of business for the past three or four years. If the records show a gradual rise in the volume of sales an attempt should be made to determine how much of the increase is due to higher prices being charged to the customers.

The next question that should be answered is, ' Is the increase in the sales due to factors internal to the establishment such as an improvement in the standard of service, advertising, etc., or is it the result of external factors over which the management has no control (for example the development of new industries in the locality, the building of new housing estates)? ' Once these questions have been answered it will be fairly easy to decide how far the past trend of business is indicative of what the sales are likely to be in the immediate future.

The main sources of published information relating to the Hotel and Catering Industry are the trade journals. These contain a great deal of information on such matters as the dividends paid by various catering businesses, new hotels and restaurants, winding-up and bankruptcies. Naturally all this information is very helpful as it has a direct bearing on the current conditions and trends in the industry.

MATERIALS BUDGET REPORT

for _____ 19_____

	CURRENT MONTH				TO DATE				ANNUAL ESTIMATES
	ESTIMATED	%	ACTUAL	%	ESTIMATED	%	ACTUAL	%	%
Meat		25				25			25
Fish and Poultry		17				17			17
Groceries		19				19			19
Fruit, Vegetables		14				14			14
Milk, Eggs, Butter		14				14			14
Bread, Rolls, etc.		7				7			7
Tea and Coffee		4				4			4
TOTALS		100				100			100
PERCENTAGES	100%				100%				

QUESTIONS AND EXERCISES FOR STUDENTS

Chapter One—Introduction

1. What do you consider to be the objects of costing?

2. What information can the caterer obtain from cost accounting as opposed to financial accounting?

3. Give examples of the various ways in which costing might assist:
   (a) the proprietor of a medium-sized hotel
   (b) the manager of an industrial canteen.

4. Of what value is cost information when:
   (a) quoting for a special function, and
   (b) planning the menu?

5. Write a short essay on the advantages of costing.

Chapter Two—The Elements of Cost

1. Explain what you understand by:
   (a) Total Cost
   (b) Kitchen Profit
   (c) Net Profit.

2. Explain why it is difficult in catering to ascertain the total cost of any one item produced. How are these difficulties overcome?

3. The following cost data have been extracted from the records of the Chiswick Park Restaurant in respect of May, 19..:

Rent and Rates	£25·50
Gas and Electricity	£11·00
Wages—Restaurant	£64·75
,, Kitchen	£57·00
Sundry Office Expenses	£14·00
Postage and Stationery	£5·50
Telephone and Insurance	£7·25
Renewals and Depreciation	£41·00
Food Cost	£225·25
Sales for May	£525·75
Number of Customers Served	2,342

You are required:

(1) To find (a) the Kitchen Profit and (b) the Net Profit for May.

(2) To calculate the cost and profit composition of each £1 sales.

(3) To find the average spending power.

(4) To calculate the average customer's contribution towards the restaurant's (a) Kitchen Profit and (b) Net Profit.

4. The A.C.E. Catering Co. Ltd. operates three restaurants and the following table shows the costs and sales of the three units for March, 19..:

Particulars	Restaurant		
	A	C	E
	£	£	£
Stock, March 1st	400	390	560
Purchases	1,200	1,140	1,840
Stock, March 31st	360	300	480

Restaurant

Particulars	A	C	E
	£	£	£
Wages	690	640	940
Rent and Rates	90	65	130
Depreciation	120	105	145
Lighting and Heating	40	35	60
Printing and Stationery	10	15	20
Postage and Telephones	25	30	50
Licences and Bank Charges	15	20	30
Repairs and Renewals	70	80	110
Cleaning Materials	10	15	20
Sundry Office Expenses	40	65	75
Sales	2,700	2,600	3,900
Number of Customers served			7,450

NOTE: Head Office expenses ignored.

You are required:

(a) To divide the total cost for each restaurant into materials (food cost), labour and overheads.

(b) To express each figure of Net Profit as a percentage of sales.

(c) To calculate, for each restaurant, the cost and profit composition of each £100 sales.

(d) To calculate, in the case of Restaurant E:
  (i) the average spending power,
  (ii) the 'average customer's' contribution towards the restaurant's Kitchen Profit and Net Profit.

5. On 31st May, 19.., the following data were extracted from the records of a college refectory. You are informed that whilst a proportion of the rent, rates and other administrative expenses is not charged to the refectory, it is intended that it should otherwise pay its own way.

Particulars	£
Stock of Provisions, May 1st	137
Purchases: Meat and Fish	207
Groceries	78
Fruit and Vegetables	119

Particulars	£
Milk, Butter, Margarine, etc.	40
Bread, Cakes, Flour, etc.	31
Tea and Coffee	26
Stock of Provisions, May 31st	153
Staff Wages	325
Electricity and Gas	26
Cleaning Materials	7
Repairs and Maintenance	28
Depreciation	14
Laundry	18
Replacements	16
Sundry Expenses	9
Sales	941
Number of Students served	*5,416*

You are required:

(a) To find the Kitchen Profit and the Net surplus or deficit for May and to express both as percentages of sales.

(b) To find the average spending power.

(c) To calculate how much the ' average student ' contributed towards:

            (i) materials
            (ii) net surplus (or deficit).

(d) To comment on your results.

6. The following cost data have been extracted from the records of Park Restaurant in respect of September, October and November, 19..:

Particulars	*Sept.*	*Oct.*	*Nov.*
	£	£	£
Opening Stock	320	310	330
Purchases of Provisions	890	860	800
Closing Stock	310	330	240
Wages	480	480	480
Rent	60	60	60
Gas and Electricity	25	30	35
Depreciation	90	90	90
Repairs and Renewals	55	30	45

Particulars	Sept. £	Oct. £	Nov. £
Sundry Expenses	30	35	30
Postage and Telephone	20	25	25
Printing and Stationery	15	10	10
Bank and Legal Charges	60	15	30
Bad Debts	—	10	20
Sales	1,950	1,925	1,845
Number of Customers Served	5,645	5,585	5,305

You are required:

(a) To show for each month the three components of cost and the Net Profit, and express each as a percentage of sales.

(b) To calculate the percentage of Kitchen Profit for each month.

(c) To find, in each case, the 'average customer's' contribution towards the restaurant's:

      (i) Kitchen Profit,
     (ii) Net Profit,
    (iii) Wages,
    (iv) Overheads.

(d) To comment on the cost information you have produced.

7. The following are the costs and sales of an industrial canteen in respect of January, February and March, 19... The intention of the management is that the canteen should be operated at a Kitchen Profit of 50 per cent. Certain overheads, e.g. rent and rates, are not charged; otherwise the canteen is expected to 'break even.'

Particulars	Jan. £	Feb. £	Mar. £
Opening Stock	75	85	80
Purchases of Provisions	320	300	315
Closing Stock	85	80	65
Wages	225	215	215
Gas	16	14	17
Electricity	15	17	13
Depreciation	35	35	35
Replacements	16	10	12

Particulars	Jan. £	Feb. £	Mar. £
Laundry	12	13	13
Cleaning Materials	5	7	5
Sundry Expenses	11	9	10
Sales	650	632	643
Number of Meals Served	4,505	4,478	4,492

You are required:
(a) To find the Kitchen Profit and the Net surplus or deficit for each month.
(b) To show the cost and surplus (or deficit) composition of each £10 sales.
(c) To find the average spending power for each month.
(d) To calculate the 'average employee's' contribution to the canteen's Kitchen Profit.
(e) To comment in brief on the cost information derived by you.

Chapter Three—Materials (Food Costs)

(1) Give a brief description of a simple system of recording the receipts and issues from the stores of a medium-sized hotel.

(2) What do you consider to be the duties and responsibilities of the storekeeper in a large industrial canteen ?

(3) What are the purposes of material costing ?   Briefly state its advantages.

(4) What do you understand by Food Cost Control ?   Give a brief description of its purpose and the methods used.

(5) It has been said that ' portion control is fortune control.' Do you agree ?

(6) Write an essay on the objects of portion control.   Name six items of equipment which, in your opinion, facilitate the standardisation of portions.

7.   The following table shows the food-cost composition and sales of the New Restaurant for the three months ended 31st March, 19...

	Jan. £	*Feb.* £	*Mar.* £
Meat	82	102	79
Fish and Poultry	122	119	125
Groceries	62	69	63
Fruit and Vegetables	96	112	103
Milk, Eggs, Butter, etc.	46	42	39
Bread, Cakes, Flour	26	22	25
Tea and Coffee	19	21	18
Takings	997	1,002	1,063
Number of Customers Served	*2,995*	*3,061*	*3,216*

You are required:
(1) To calculate each month's food cost and Kitchen Profit, expressing each figure as a percentage of sales.
(2) To express each group of provisions as a percentage of sales.
(3) To find each month's average spending power.
(4) To comment on the composition of each month's food cost.

8. The following are the ingredients necessary to produce 5 litres of potage Esaü (lentil soup garnished with rice, served with croûtons).

1 kg lentils	@ 20p per kg
½ kg carrots	@ 9p ,, ,,
0·150 kg onions	@ 13p ,, ,,
½ kg bacon bones	@ 15p ,, ,,
0·050 kg rice	@ 15p ,, ,,
0·150 kg margarine	@ 30p ,, ,,
1 small white loaf	@ 8p ,, ,,

You are required:
(a) To find the total cost of ingredients.
(b) To give the average food cost per portion, assuming 1 litre = 5 portions.
(c) To calculate the percentage Kitchen Profit, assuming that all the portions are sold at:
      (i) 4p per portion.
     (ii) 5p ,, ,,
    (iii) 6p ,, ,,

9. The following list shows the ingredients required to produce 5 litres of crème Dubarry (cream of cauliflower soup served with croûtons):

2½ l milk	@ 18p per litre
2½ l white stock—estimated cost	15p
0·400 kg margarine	@ 30p per kg

0·250 kg flour	@ 6p ,, ,,
0·050 kg onions	@ 13p ,, ,,
2 medium-sized cauliflowers	@ 50p per litre
¼ l single cream	@ 50p ,, ,,
1 small white loaf	@ 8p

(a) Assuming 1 litre of soup=5 portions, find the cost of ingredients for 120 portions.
(b) Calculate the average cost per portion.
(c) What would have to be the selling price per portion if it were desired to achieve a Kitchen Profit of 75 per cent?

10. The following are the ingredients necessary to produce 10 portions of sole Colbert (whole Dover sole, egg and bread-crumbed, deep fried, served with parsley, butter, quarters of lemon, fried parsley):

10 × ½ kg Dover soles	@ £1·40 per kg
0·300 kg flour	@ 6p ,, ,,
3 eggs	@ 1½p each
1 large stale loaf—say	2p
1 bunch parsley	@ 5p
0·200 kg butter	@ 52p per kg
3 lemons	@ 4p each
5 l frying oil	@ 25p per litre
(assume absorption=6%)	

You are required to find:
(a) Total food cost.
(b) The average cost per portion.
(c) The selling price per portion, assuming a Kitchen Profit of:
      (i) 55 per cent.
     (ii) 60 ,, ,,
    (iii) 65 ,, ,,

(d) The average cost per portion, assuming that the price
    of Dover sole is:
    (i) £1·30 per kg
    (ii) £1·20 ,, ,,
    (iii) £1·10 ,, ,, and there is no change in the
    prices of other ingredients.

11. The following are necessary to produce 10 portions of
sole Veronique (whole Dover sole poached, served with white
wine sauce, garnished with pealed grapes and puff pastry
flourons):

10 × ½ kg Dover soles	@	£1·40 per kg
1 bottle white wine	@	50p
½ kg butter	@	52p per kg
¼ l single cream	@	50p per litre
¼ l double cream	@	70p ,, ,,
0·350 kg grapes	@	30p per kg
0·100 kg flour	@	6p ,, ,,

You are required:
(a) To calculate (i) total food cost, (ii) the average cost per
    portion.
(b) Find the selling price per portion, assuming a Kitchen
    profit of
        (i) 66 per cent.
        (ii) 60 ,,   ,,

(c) Show the effect on the average cost per portion of a
    decrease in the price paid for the sole to:
        (i) £1·30 per kg
        (ii) £1·20 ,, ,,

12. The following ingredients are necessary to produce 10
portions of filet de sole bonne femme (poached with fish
stock, white wine, chopped parsley, chopped shallots and
sliced mushrooms; served with above garnish and sauce made
from cooking liquor, butter, cream and eggs):

5 × ½ kg Dover soles	@	£1·40 per kg
½ kg onions	@	13p ,, ,,
1 bunch parsley	@	5p
0·070 shallots	@	20p per kg
½ kg button mushrooms	@	50p ,, ,,
1 bottle white wine	@	50p
0·200 kg butter	@	52p per kg
¼ l double cream	@	70p per litre
3 eggs	@	1½p each

You are required:
(a) To find the cost of ingredients for 50 portions.
(b) To find the average food cost per portion.
(c) To calculate the Kitchen Profit on these 50 portions
   sold at:

        (i) 55 per cent Kitchen Profit,
       (ii) 60 ,,   ,,   ,,   ,,
      (iii) 65 ,,   ,,   ,,   ,,

13.   You require the following ingredients to produce 10
portions of Irish stew:

1¼ kg middle neck of lamb	@	35p per kg
1¼ kg potatoes	@	4p ,, ,,
0·200 kg onions	@	13p ,, ,,
2 leeks—estimated cost		10p
1 small head of celery	@	10p
¼ kg button onions	@	18p per kg
1 small bunch of parsley	@	5p

You are required to calculate:
(a) The total cost of ingredients used. → 0·811   (81p)
(b) The average cost per portion.   → ÷10 = 0·0811
(c) The percentage Kitchen Profit, assuming that the selling
   price is:
        (i) 14p per portion   0·059 (5·9p)
       (ii) 16p ,,   ,,   0·077 (7·9p)
      (iii) 18p ,,   ,,   0·099 (9·9p)

14. The following ingredients are required to produce 10 portions of poussin rôti au lard:

10 single poussins	@ 35p each
0·200 kg white lard	@ 22p per kg
0·200 kg streaky bacon	@ 30p ,, ,,
½ kg potatoes	@ 4p ,, ,,
2 bunches watercress	@ 6p each
0·100 kg bread—cost	11p
1 button onion—say	½p
1 l brown stock—cost	7p
¼ l milk	@ 12p per litre

(a) What is the food cost of the 10 portions?
(b) What is the average cost per portion?
(c) Calculate the selling price per portion, assuming a Kitchen Profit of:

> (i) 55 per cent.
> (ii) 60 ,, ,,
> (iii) 65 ,, ,,

15. The ingredients necessary to produce 20 portions of crêpes au citron are as follows:

1 l milk	@ 12p per litre
½ kg flour	@ 5p per kg
4 eggs	@ 1½p each
0·600 kg castor sugar	@ 12p per kg
4 lemons	@ 4p each

(a) Find the cost of ingredients for 50 portions.
(b) Find the average cost per portion.
(c) What would be the average cost per portion if the price of eggs were:

> (i) 1p each
> (ii) 1¼p ,,
> (iii) 1¾p ,,
> (iv) 2p ,,   ?

16.   The ingredients necessary to produce 20 portions of
crème caramel are:

2 l milk	@ 12p per litre
12 large eggs	@ 2p each
0·300 kg granulated sugar	@ 12p per kg
1 vanilla stick	@ 9p
1 kg lump sugar	@ 12p per kg

(a) Find the cost of ingredients for 50 portions.
(b) Calculate the average cost per portion.
(c) Show the average cost per portion when the price of
    large eggs is:

> (i) $1\frac{1}{2}$p each
> (ii) $1\frac{1}{4}$p ,,
> (iii) $2\frac{1}{4}$p ,,

17.   The ingredients necessary to produce 10 portions of
flan aux pommes are as follows:

0·300 kg flour	@ 5p per kg
0·150 kg margarine	@ 30p ,, ,,
0·070 kg sugar	@ 10p ,, ,,
2 eggs	@ $1\frac{1}{2}$p each
$1\frac{3}{4}$ kg cooking apples	@ 20 p per kg
1 lemon	@ 4p
0·200 kg granulated sugar	@ 12p per kg
0·200 kg apricot jam	@ 17p ,, ,,

(a) Find the cost of ingredients for 25 portions.
(b) Calculate the average cost per portion.
(c) What would be the Kitchen Profit earned if the 25
    portions were sold at:

> (i) 5p per portion
> (ii) 6p ,,   ,,
> (iii) 7p ,,   ,,   ?

18.   The following menu is to be prepared for one hundred
covers

GRAPEFRUIT COCKTAIL
FILET DE SOLE BERCY
DINDONNEAUX ROTIS AUX CHIPOLATAS
POMMES CHATEAU
BOUTONS DE CHOUX DE BRUXELLES AU BEURRE
CHARLOTTE RUSSE
CAFÉ

The ingredients you require are:

Grapefruit cocktail:	70 large seedless grapefruits
	2 large bottles maraschino cherries
Filet de sole bercy:	$25 \times \frac{1}{2}$ kg Dover soles
	12 eggs
	$\frac{1}{2}$ l single cream
	$\frac{1}{2}$ kg shallots
	$\frac{1}{2}$ kg onions
	2 lemons
	1 bunch parsley
	2 bottles white wine
	1 kg butter
	0·100 kg margarine
	0·200 kg plain flour
Dindonneaux rôtis aux chipolatas:	3 kg chipolatas
	3×7 kg turkeys
	10 bunches watercress
	$1\frac{1}{2}$ kg dripping (absorption and waste $= 50\%$)
	2 l brown stock
Bread sauce and stuffing:	2 l milk
	6 eggs
	1 kg onions
	2 lemons
	$1\frac{1}{2}$ l thyme
	4 small white loaves
	$\frac{1}{2}$ kg suet

Pommes château	17 kg potatoes
	1 bunch parsley
	1 kg dripping (absorption and waste = 50%)
	½ kg butter
Boutons de choux de bruxelles:	15 kg button Brussel sprouts
	1 kg butter
Charlotte russe:	4 l milk
	35 eggs
	2 l single cream
	2 l double cream
	2 vanilla sticks
	2 kg granulated sugar
	¼ kg sheet gelatine
Lady fingers:	16 eggs
	½ kg castor sugar
	½ kg plain flour
Café	7½ l milk
	1 kg ground coffee
	2 kg Demerara sugar

Find current market prices for the above ingredients and calculate:

(a) the total food cost of the menu,
(b) the average food cost per cover.

19.   You are required to prepare the following menu for one hundred covers:

CRÈME PALESTINE

FILET DE PLIE FRITE, SAUCE TARTARE

POULET ROTI AU LARD

POMMES RISSOLEES

PETITS POIS A LA MENTHE

POUDING SOUFFLE AU CITRON

CAFÉ

The following list shows the ingredients required:

Crème Palestine:	7 l milk
	1 l single cream
	5 kg Jerusalem artichokes
	2 lemons
	1 kg margarine
	$\frac{1}{2}$ kg plain flour
	12 l white stock
Croûtons	$\frac{1}{2}$ l oil
	0·200 kg butter
	1 small stale loaf
Filet de plie frite:	100 × 0·100 kg fillets of plaice
	12 eggs
	3 small stale loaves
	1 kg plain flour
	$\frac{1}{10}$ l olive oil
	15 l cooking oil (absorption and waste=10%)
Sauce tartare:	9 eggs
	1 bunch parsley
	$1\frac{3}{4}$ l olive oil
	0·030 kg mustard
	$\frac{1}{2}$ l vinegar
	2 jars capers
	2 jars gherkins
Poulet rôti au lard:	25 × 1·200 kg chickens
	$2\frac{1}{4}$ kg streaky bacon
	$2\frac{1}{4}$ l milk
	$2\frac{1}{4}$ kg potatoes
	0·100 kg onions
	10 bunches watercress
	2 small white loaves
	$2\frac{1}{4}$ kg lard (absorption and waste=10%)
	$2\frac{1}{4}$ l brown stock

Pommes rissolées:
17 kg potatoes
1 bunch parsley
1 kg dripping (absorption and waste=50%)
½ kg butter

Petits pois à la menthe:
9 kg frozen peas
3 bunches mint

Pouding soufflé au citron:
6 l milk
50 eggs
12 lemons
2¼ kg sugar
1 kg flour
1 kg butter
½ kg margarine
¾ kg granulated sugar
0·060 kg custard powder

Crème Anglaise:
3 l milk
20 eggs
¾ kg granulated sugar
0·060 kg custard powder

Café
9 l milk
¾ kg ground coffee
1¾ kg Demerara sugar

You are required to calculate:
(a) The total food cost of the menu.
(b) The average food cost of each item.
(c) The average food cost per cover. Use a Portion Costing Sheet for your calculations.

Chapter Four—Labour

(1) Explain what is meant by the ' inclusive ' cost of labour.

(2) Draft a time-sheet and indicate its usefulness in the preparation of the pay-roll.

(3) What do you understand by labour-turnover? What are the main effects of a high rate of labour-turnover?

(4) What are the factors determining the extent to which labour may be replaced by labour-saving devices?

(5) Indicate the main effects of the fixity of wage costs.

(6) Name six items of equipment which are, in your opinion, labour-saving.

(7) Give ten examples of dishes which are fairly inexpensive on terms of food cost, but costly in terms of labour.

Chapter Five—Overheads

(1) Explain what is meant by the term ' overheads.'

(2) What are the main methods of depreciation ? Discuss their advantages and disadvantages.

(3) Explain what is meant by:
    (a) Capital expenditure,
    (b) Revenue expenditure,
    (c) Scrap value.

(4) What do you consider to be the best method of controlling the following items of expense:
    (a) Cleaning materials,
    (b) Postage,
    (c) Renewals,
    (d) Linen,
    (e) Cutlery,
    (f) Gas.

(5) State, with reasons, which method of depreciation you would adopt for each of the following assets:
    (a) Electric potato-peeler,
    (b) China,
    (c) Cutlery,
    (d) Ice-cream servers,
    (e) Tea measuring machine,
    (f) Leasehold premises,
    (g) Linen.

(6) What do you consider to be the most important advantages of a monthly overheads cost analysis ?

Chapter six—Profit

(1) Show the distinction between Kitchen Profit and Net Profit.

(2) What do you understand by the ' elements of profit ' ?

(3) What are the main factors determining the percentage of Kitchen Profit—
    (a) on different items of food,
    (b) in different types of catering establishment ?

(4) Explain why the Net Profit earned by the caterer is indicative of his success or otherwise in business.

(5) Show, by means of a numerical example, the relationship between the volume of business and the Net Profit earned.

(6) Explain the difference between fixed and variable costs.

(7) The following is a summary of the trading account of the Creswick Restaurant for the first year of its operation.

		£	£
Sales	Food	40,000	
	Drink	20,000	60,000
Less Variable Costs:	Food	20,000	
	Drink	8,000	
	Other	2,000	30,000
			30,000
Less Fixed Costs			25,000
Net Profit			5,000

The proprietor expects that during the second year the volume of sales will increase by 10 per cent. Food and beverage costs are likely to increase by 8 per cent. and

other variable costs by 15 per cent. No change is expected
in the fixed costs of the restaurant.

Prepare an estimated trading account for the second
year of the restaurant's operation.

(8) A restaurant serves up to 10,000 covers per month. The
average spending power is 50p. Variable costs are equal
to 50 per cent. of the volume of sales and fixed costs
amount to £1,500 per month. Prepare a break-even chart
of the restaurant, indicating clearly the break-even point.

Chapter Seven—Price Policy

(1) What are the main objections to the food cost-plus-Kitchen Profit method of pricing?

(2) Give a short outline of the factors that would have to be taken into account when fixing the price of an item to be included in an *à la carte* menu.

(3) Do you consider that there should be any difference in the price policy of a medium-sized hotel and a medium-sized restaurant, having regard to the fact that most of the hotel's revenue is derived from the sale of accommodation ?

(4) The price paid by the customer must be such as to cover the three elements of cost and leave a sufficient margin of Net Profit. Explain how the caterer's price policy depends on the cost and profit composition of his sales.

Chapter Eight—Budgetary Control

(1) Explain what you understand by budgetary control.

(2) Write a short essay on the purposes and advantages of budgeting.

(3) Write notes on the following:
    (a) The Budget Period.
    (b) The Determination of Costs.

(4) The following information is extracted from the books of a non-seasonal, licensed restaurant:

	Food	Wines and Spirits	Cigars and Cigarettes
	£	£	£
Sales in Year 1	19,860	3,450	1,020
Year 2	20,850	4,140	1,070
Year 3	22,940	4,350	1,100
Year 4	24,750	4,610	1,160

Having regard to the past trend of sales and current circumstances, it is estimated that in Year 5 the sales will increase as follows: (a) Food 10%; (b) Wines and Spirits 6%; (c) Cigars and Cigarettes 4%.

You are required to calculate the estimated annual and monthly sales in Year 5.

At the end of January in Year 5, it was found that actual sales for that month were:
    (a) Food   £2,450
    (b) Wines and Spirits   £450
    (c) Cigars and Cigarettes £96

Prepare a Monthly Sales Budget Report for January.

(5) The following are the annual budget estimates for 19..:

Meat	£2,237·50	25%
Fish and Poultry	£1,521·50	17%
Fruit, Vegetables and Groceries	£2,953·50	33%
Milk, Eggs, Butter	£1,253·00	14%
Bread, Rolls, etc.	£626·50	7%
Tea and Coffee	358·00	4%
	£8,950·00	100%

Calculate monthly food cost estimates.

The following figures show the actual consumption of food:

	January	February
Meat	£164·50	£182·09
Fish and Poultry	£148·13	£127·75
Fruit, Vegetables and Groceries	£256·00	£229·55
Milk, Eggs, Butter	£112·00	£99·50
Bread, Rolls, etc.	£48·75	£54·55
Tea and Coffee	£30·00	£27·95

You are required to prepare a Monthly Materials Budget Report for January and February.

(6) What do you consider to be the likely effect of a 10 per cent. increase in the volume of a hotel's sales on the following items of expense:

    (a) Food Cost
    (b) Insurance
    (c) Depreciation
    (d) Printing and Stationery
    (e) Wages and National Insurance
    (f) Rates
    (g) Lighting and Heating
    (h) Laundry?

FURTHER READING

Food Cost Control by R. Kotas and B. Davis, Intertext Books.
Control in Catering by James Steel, Barrie and Jenkins.
A Standard System of Catering Accounting by the Hotel and
Catering E.D.C., H.M.S.O.
Profitable Food and Beverage Operation by J. Brodner, H. M.
Carlson and H. T. Mashall, Ahrens.